What's in this book

This book belongs to

_____

新邻居 The new neighbour

学习内容 Contents

沟通 Communication

说出月份和日期
Say the months and dates

数一至三十一
Count from one to 31

生词 New words

★ 一月	January	★ 十月	October
★ 二月	February	★ 十一月	November
★ 三月	March	★ 十二月	December
★ 四月	April	★ 月	month, moon
★ 五月	May	★ 日	date, day
★ 六月	June	燕子	swallow
★ 七月	July	来	to come
★ 八月	August	回来	to come back
★ 九月	September		

背景介绍：
春天的某一天，浩浩和玲玲惊讶地发现自家院子的树上出现了一个鸟巢。

Get ready

1 What is in the tree?

2 What is it for?

3 Have you seen a real one before?

我们用"X 月 Y 日"来表达具体的月份和日期，如"四月四日"。其中，一年有 12 个月，故 X 从"一"到"十二"；每个月最多 31 天，故 Y 从"一"到"三十一"。在中文里，先说"X 月"，再说"Y 日"。

sì　yuè
四月

四	日	一	二	三	四	五	六	月
		1	2	3	4	5	6	
			9	10	11	12	13	
			17	18	19	20		
			25	26	27			

故事大意：
春天到了，浩浩和玲玲发现燕子们在自家院子的树上筑巢、生活、学习飞翔。十月秋天到了，燕子们飞往南方过冬。第二年春天，燕子们又回来了。

四月四日，燕子来我们家了。

参考问题和答案：

1 What do you think Dad is saying to Hao Hao and Ling Ling?
   (The birds outside the window are swallows.)

2 When did the swallows come to Hao Hao's home? (4 April.)

liù yuè
六月

六月九日，小燕子学会飞了。

参考问题和答案：

1 What are the young swallows doing? (They are being taught how to fly by their parents.)
2 When is this happening? (9 June.)

十 月

shí yuè

十 月 八 日 ， 燕 子 不 见 了 。

参考问题和答案：

1 What season is it? (It is autumn.)

2 When is this? (8 October.)

3 What happened? (The swallows have gone.)

4 How do Hao Hao and Ling Ling look? (They look worried and disappointed.)

燕子回家了，明年再来。

参考问题和答案：

1　What do you think Dad says to Hao Hao and Ling Ling? (The swallows have gone home.)
2　What is Hao Hao thinking about? (He has a vision of the swallows gathering in the south where it is warm.)

shí yī yuè
十一月

shí èr yuè
十二月

十一月、十二月……
燕子快回来！

参考问题和答案：

1　What season is it? (It is winter.)

2　Are the swallows here in November and December? (No, they are not.)

四月又到了，燕子回来了！

参考问题和答案：

1 What season is it? (It is spring again.)
2 Which month is it? (It is April.)
3 Have the swallows finally come back? (Yes, they have.)
4 How do Hao Hao and Ling Ling look? (They look happy and excited.)

Let's think

1 Recall the story and number the pictures in order. Write in Chinese. 提醒学生回忆故事，结合图中季节、燕子和燕巢的变化来排序，并注意要书写汉字。

二

三

一

四

2 Discuss with your friend.

以燕子为代表的候鸟，每年会在固定季节成群进行有规律的迁徙活动，从而适应环境变化，利于物种生存繁衍。类似的还有鱼类洄游和哺乳动物的迁徙等。

What does Dad say when the swallows fly away?

参考答案：
The swallows fly south for the winter, and will come back next spring.

Where have the swallows gone?

参考答案：
They have gone somewhere warmer and with more food.

New words

延伸活动：
老师先让学生练习说出一月到十二月，及一日到三十一日。
再任意指向日历上的日期，由学生说出来。

1 Learn the new words.

月

三月

日

燕子

来

回来

Sun	Mon	Tue	Wed	Thur	Fri	Sat
		一	二	三	四	五
六	七	八	九	十	十一	十二
十三	十四	十五	十六	十七	十八	十九
二十	二十一	二十二	二十三	二十四	二十五	二十六
二十七	二十八	二十九	三十	三十一		

"来"是指动作向自己（说话人）靠近的这一过程。"回来"表示从其他地方回到原地。

2 When are these festivals? Circle the correct answers.

1

圣诞节：十二月二十五日

a 六月
b 十月
ⓒ 十二月

2

新年（元旦）：一月一日

ⓐ 一日
b 十五日
c 二十日

听听说说 Listen and say

1 Listen and colour the eggs.

提醒学生给答案涂色。

日	六	十九
我	十八	再
十五	二	十一
狗	二十	十三
四	弟	十六
岁	十四	三
七你	字眼	头月

2 Look at the pictures. Listen to t

再见！我十月
十五日回来！

爸爸回来了！

ory and say.

 **3** Listen and circle the correct answers.

1 When does Mum come home?

a 四月 16

b 四月 1

2 When does Hao Hao go to school?

a 九月 13

b 九月 20

Task

Colour the months according to the instructions. Say the months in each colour group. 先让学生整体认读并复习一月到十二月，再让学生根据题目要求给每个月份涂上相应的颜色。提醒学生粉色的月份都有 31 日，绿色的月份都有 30 日，蓝色的二月有 28 日或 29 日。

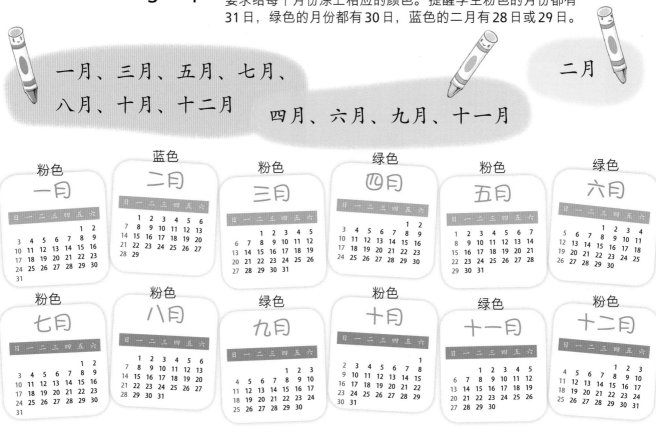

一月、三月、五月、七月、八月、十月、十二月

四月、六月、九月、十一月

二月

Game

Find out your friends' birthdays and write them down. Colour the balloon. 提醒学生用汉字来写日期，填写完再给气球上色。

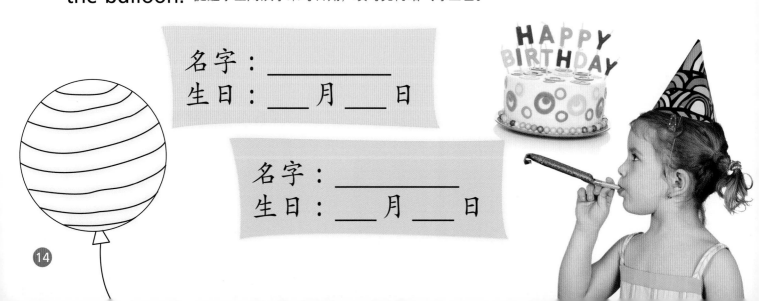

名字：＿＿＿＿＿
生日：＿＿月＿＿日

名字：＿＿＿＿＿
生日：＿＿月＿＿日

Song

Listen and sing.

延伸活动：
让学生看图并说说图中的事情分别发生在哪个月。然后老师指定某一顺序（如教室里的某一横排，或竖排，或顺时针等），让学生们按该顺序依次唱出十二个月份。

一月二月三四月，
五月六月七八月，
九月十月十一月，
十二月后又一月。

课堂用语 Classroom language

知道吗？

Do you know?

明白吗？

Do you understand?

做完了吗？

Have you finished?

15

写一写 Write

1 Learn and trace the stroke. 老师示范笔画动作，学生跟着做：用手在空中画出"横折钩"。

横折钩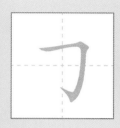

2 Learn the component. Circle 月 in the characters.

提醒学生，"月"既是部件也是独体字，它像又长又弯的月亮，中间两横分别是月亮的眼睛和嘴巴。

3 Chang'e lives on the moon. Colour her home.

温柔貌美的嫦娥是后羿的妻子。她为了保持年轻，偷吃西王母的不死药而奔月。此后一直居住在月亮上。

4 Trace and write the character.

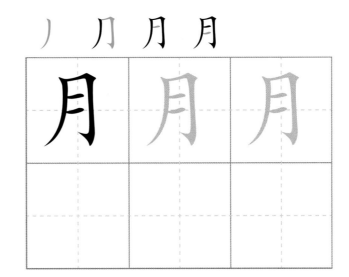

丿 刀 月 月

 **Did you know?**

象形字由形象的图画发展而来，即用线条或笔画，勾画出事物的特征。经过简化和发展，形成了今天所使用的部分文字。

Some characters have developed from pictures of people or things which give clues to their meanings.

山

Guess what these characters mean. Write the letters.

 a 耳   b 人   c 燕

 b

a

c

Cultures

1 Learn about the difference between the solar calendar and the Chinese lunar calendar.

"农历"在中国及东南亚地区广泛使用，很多重要的节日，如农历新年、元宵节和中秋节等，都是按农历来计算的。

> The solar calendar is based on the movement of the earth around the sun.

> The Chinese lunar calendar is based on the cycles of the lunar phases.

APRIL

Sunday	Monday	Tuesday	Wednesday	Thursday	Friday	Saturday
		1	2	3	4	5
1	2	3	4	10	11	12
13	14	15	16	17	18	19
20	21	22	23	24	25	26
27	28	29	30			

四月

一	二	三	四	五	六	日
		初一	初二	初三	初四	初五
初六	初七	初八	初九	初十	十一	十二
十三	十四	十五	十六	十七	十八	十九
二十	廿一	廿二	廿三	廿四	廿五	廿六
廿七	廿八	廿九	三十			

2 Use paper plates to show phases of the moon.

> 一月……十二月十五

所需材料：一把剪刀、一支铅笔、四个白色纸盘。
先用铅笔在第一个纸盘上画出第一个月亮的形状后剪下，剩余部分即第三个月亮。再用第二个纸盘重复此步骤，分别作为第七个、第五个月亮。然后把第三个纸盘剪成一半，分别作为第二个、第六个月亮。第四个月亮则是一个完整的纸盘。最后将剪好的月亮进行排序，展现其阴晴变化。

Project

1 Make your own calendar.

参照其他完整日历，在空白日历本填上月份和日期。

在完成的日历上标注节日、自己的生日，或者其它重要的日子。

2 Play a guessing game. Say the dates of the festivals your friends show.

三人一组，其中两人用动作表现某节日的特色，一人在日历上指出该节日并说出来。

建议日期：一月一日（新年）、四月一日（愚人节）和十二月二十五日（圣诞节）等。

十月三十一日！

温习 Checkpoint

游戏方法：
从底部大门开始，依次闯关回答问题。每完成一个问
题，即可进入门内上升一步，直到完成所有问题后才
可见到最上方的嫦娥。

1 Follow the instruction on each gate to meet the beautiful Chang'e in the moon palace.

Write 'moon' in Chinese.

月

Say the password 279613 in Chinese.

二七九六一三

Say your birthday in Chinese.

Say '15 August' in Chinese.

八月十五日

Read the month.

十一月

评核方法：
学生两人一组，互相考察评价表内单词和句子的听说读写。交际沟通部分由老师朗读要求，学生再互相对话。如果达到了某项技能要求，则用色笔将星星或小辣椒涂色。

2 Work with your friend. Colour the stars and the chillies.

Words	说	读	写
一月	☆	☆	☆
二月	☆	☆	☆
三月	☆	☆	☆
四月	☆	☆	🌶
五月	☆	☆	🌶
六月	☆	☆	☆
七月	☆	☆	🌶
八月	☆	☆	☆
九月	☆	☆	🌶
十月	☆	☆	☆
十一月	☆	☆	☆
十二月	☆	☆	☆

Words and sentences	说	读	写
月	☆	☆	☆
日	☆	☆	☆
燕子	☆	🌶	🌶
来	☆	🌶	🌶
回来	☆	🌶	🌶
四月四日，燕子来我们家了。	☆	🌶	🌶

Say the months and dates	☆
Count from one to 31	☆

3 What does your teacher say?

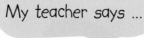
My teacher says ...

评核建议：
根据学生课堂表现，分别给予"太棒了！(Excellent!)"、"不错！(Good!)"或"继续努力！(Work harder!)"的评价，再让学生圈出上方对应的表情，以记录自己的学习情况。

分享 Sharing

Words I remember

一月	yī yuè	January	十月	shí yuè	
二月	èr yuè	February	十一月	shí yī yu
三月	sān yuè	March	十二月	shí èr yu
四月	sì yuè	April	月	yuè
五月	wǔ yuè	May	日	rì
六月	liù yuè	June	燕子	yàn zi
七月	qī yuè	July	来	lái
八月	bā yuè	August	回来	huí lái
九月	jiǔ yuè	September		

Other words

这	zhè	this
家	jiā	home
学会	xué huì	to have learned
飞	fēi	to fly
明年	míng nián	next year
快	kuài	hurry, soon
又	yòu	again
到	dào	to come, to arrive
了	le	(modal particle to indicate a change of status)

ctober

ovember

ecember

onth, moon

ate, day

vallow

o come

o come back

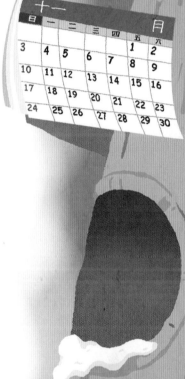

延伸活动：
1 学生用手遮盖英文，读中文单词，并思考单词意思；
2 学生用手遮盖中文单词，看着英文说出对应的中文单词；
3 学生三人一组，尽量运用中文单词分角色复述故事。

OXFORD
UNIVERSITY PRESS

Oxford University Press is a department of the University of Oxford.
It furthers the University's objective of excellence in research, scholarship,
and education by publishing worldwide. Oxford is a registered trade mark of
Oxford University Press in the UK and in certain other countries

Published in Hong Kong by
Oxford University Press (China) Limited
39th Floor, One Kowloon, 1 Wang Yuen Street, Kowloon Bay,
Hong Kong

© Oxford University Press (China) Limited 2017

The moral rights of the author have been asserted

First Edition published in 2017

Illustrated by Anne Lee and Wildman

Photographs for reproduction permitted by Dreamstime.com

China National Publications Import & Export (Group) Corporation is an authorized distributor of
Oxford Elementary Chinese.

Please contact content@cnpiec.com.cn or 86-10-65856782

ISBN: 978-0-19-082141-8

10 9 8 7 6 5 4 3 2

Teacher's Edition
ISBN: 978-0-19-082153-1

10 9 8 7 6 5 4 3 2